MW00586745

So Okay...

TREASURED STORIES FROM THE LIFE OF

JAMES M. ROBINSON, SR.

AS TOLD TO

C.L. FAILS

LaunchCrate
PUBLISHING

LaunchCrate Publishing
clfails@launchcrate.com
www.launchcrate.com

Ordering Information:
Quantity sales. Special discounts are available on quantity purchases by corporations, associations, and others. For details, contact the publisher at the email address above. Orders by U.S. trade bookstores and wholesalers.

Library of Congress Control Number: 2017905812

ISBN 978-0-9886689-6-6 (hardcover)
ISBN 978-0-9886689-8-0 (ebook)

Printed in the United States of America
10 9 8 7 6 5 4 3 2 1

First Edition

This book is dedicated to Grandpa James, his children, grandchildren, great-grandchildren, and all family who are yet to come, his friends, extended family, colleagues, fellow soldiers, and all who crossed his path; thank you for sharing his stories with others. His life's work lives on through you.

Table of
Contents

Table of
Contents

About this Book
On Life's Journey

Whether he realized it or not, my grandfather has inspired me with a handful of ideas to keep on the forefront of my mind as I continue to navigate through the world. My hope in sharing these stories is that at least one will resonate with you and leave a lasting impression so deep that you share it with at least one other person. In addition to sharing these stories via print, I have also captured his voice so you can hear the story and all of our playful banter direct from him.

Each section that shares an eligible Grandpa James story will contain a QR code for you to scan with your smartphone or tablet to listen to the audio. To access these bonus audio files, find a free and reliable QR code reader for your phone or internet accessible tablet.

The first QR code can be found in the Introduction so find and

So Okay...

download your preferred QR reader now and practice with the first story before you get too far into the book. When you're prepared to scan the audio, move on to the Introduction where you'll find more information about the origin of this book. I hope you enjoy it as much as I enjoyed piecing it together!

Introduction
So okay...

...I have been listening to my grandpa's stories since I was a kid. I have also been on more road trips to tiny Dalton, MO than you could shake a stick at. Some of those visits were with my parents. Most of them though - at least to my recollection, occurred between the ages of 3 and 5 while riding in the back of a car I knew only as "Big Orange," Grandpa's tangerine colored 1972 Oldsmobile Ninety-Eight Sedan. It was during these trips that I heard the most stories.

Dalton, being just a short day trip from Kansas City, was close enough that we could ride there and back while my parents were at work. The two hour ride to Dalton was long enough to get in a few really good stories about what it was like when he was a youngster. Though I couldn't envision him as a kid when I was one myself, I could see him as an adult letting a hog loose in the high school and the thought of a wild pig bumbling through hallway after hallway just cracked me up. Take a listen for yourself. Scan the first of several QR codes to hear about *Grandpa James and The Wild Hog* (or read the transcript of this story below).

Grandpa James and The Wild Hog

"It was snow. I says, 'I believe I'll put that ole hog in the school.' She says, 'I bet you won't!' I said, 'okay'. We run the ole hog around to the back of the school. I caught 'em! See, cause the snow was so deep he couldn't hardly make it, see. So I hold him there and got a snowball and throwed it up to the window. The boys up there got one little booger and took him by his heels and stuck him down there and he got hold to the hog and they pulled him and the hog both in there and set the hog in a chair. You know, one of those chairs with a desk on it. I forgot about that! The hog, he fell outta the chair and messed up everything. You know when he got scared he start doing everything. So they got the agriculture boys to get him out and clean up. I didn't even have to do that. So the teacher asked me, she says, 'Mr. Robinson, what do you think should happen to anybody that puts a hog like that in school?' I says, 'Mrs. Jackson, that was a bad boy wasn't it?' She says, 'You was the one!' I said, 'How'd you know it was me?' She says, 'I saw you running the hog!'...I was a booger!"

In Dalton, I would entertain myself by coloring on something I had packed in my Snoopy totebag, while Grandpa and his siblings or former neighbors would spin more stories. I always knew it would be a good one when he would start with the phrase, "So okay...". I didn't know what story he was about to tell but I did know that it would end in laughter. So I would color and patiently wait for the impending guffaw and then giggle because they were cracking up. Hey, when you're young, it doesn't take much. Don't believe me? Just say the word "poot" to a child and see what happens. The thing is, with Grandpa's stories, you didn't need any off color humor. The events themselves were fascinating enough - I mean, stockpiling rocks on a bus to protect yourselves from stone-slinging bigots. Who wouldn't be intrigued by that story? We all were.

I am one of 11 grandchildren and in birth order I land squarely in the middle of the pack so I know that my experience with Grandpa's stories is far from unique. All eleven of us have listened to his stories many times over, as have each of his 8 children and their spouses. He has traded stories with 11 siblings, and has shared them with countless friends, extended family, co-workers and sometimes strangers. I love listening to his stories and as time progressed I have found myself more re-energized by them each time we added a new member to our growing family. Funny thing about time though, the more it passes by the less we tend to remember, which brings me to the point of this book.

Initially it started as a gift to current and future generations of our family - a way to document those stories that we've all heard a million times and still cherish. What I found along the way, as I sat and listened to my grandpa share his stories this time around, is that there is a much greater narrative to be heard; one of a universal human experience.

Today as I write this, my grandfather, a Buffalo Solider, WWII Vet, Post Office retiree, and wild hog captor, is 94 years old and still driving himself to church every Sunday. He has quite a story to tell and as you might imagine, he has led an extremely complex life - spanning the times of horse and buggy through self-driving cars. He has experienced, much like you and I are doing now, many of the highs and lows of life - from the birth of his children and watching them soar, to a commitment to survive through the deaths of his parents, all but one sibling, the love of his life, and his first born son.

Through it all, the man who was 43 years old when the Voting Rights Act of 1965 was passed, has found a way to persist through life without allowing the trials to usurp his triumphs. This book, which initially sought to solely capture his treasured stories, now serves to dually provide some of Grandpa's handy advice about navigating through life. May it bring value to you or someone you care about.

Chapter 1
On Childhood

He sits in his recliner, dressed in a button-up shirt and overalls, silver hair peeking out from underneath his ball cap. His aviator eyeglasses frame his face and rest easy upon the bridge of his nose. The only facial hair you'll find is a perfectly trimmed "Dalton Mustache"; snipped to the corners of his mouth and missing all hair in the philtrum - you know, that vertical groove that extends from the base of your nose to the upper border of your lip. To his left, an old end table with mail, a lamp, remote controls and other "necessities" just in case. Behind him a black upright piano cloaked in baseball caps. In front of him, a folding tray table with today's newspapers, a jug of water, a pad of paper and pen for him to jot down notes, and the digital voice recorder I've placed in front of him to help me document the stories of his life.

"You haven't got this on yet?" he asks.

"Yes, it's on," I reply.

"Turn it off first and we'll get ourselves situated," he finishes. I comply.

We share much more than blood. Grandpa and I in this moment both want to get this right. So we work together to get organized and begin again. This is the first in more than a month's worth of interviews I would conduct to gather his life story. He was nervous and so was I. But the pursuit of capturing his stories was important to me, and seemed even more so to him.

We start at the beginning as he tells me more about when and where he was born. He began slowly:

> "I was born in Dalton, Missourah. September the nineteenth, nineteen, twenty-two. Dalton is on the Missouri river and is near a place where when the river would get high, we would have floods. So a lot of people moved into town where they wouldn't have floods."

He described the elementary schools in the north, south, and in town, plus four years of high school - all black. The sixteen or so white children that lived in Dalton, MO traveled about five and a half miles northeast to Keytesville to attend school; not uncommon for the times. In fact, the desegregation ruling of Brown v. Board of Ed. wouldn't occur until Grandpa was nearly 34 years old. Dalton, like many other small towns in America at the time, couldn't make adjustments that sustained its existence, closing the doors of Dalton Vocational High School just 7 years later and sending its students to finish their education with the white students in Keytesville.

Though the last population count on record was only 16, when he was younger, Dalton was a bustling town of around 1300 people.

> "There used to be stores all along there. Just one store hooked to another. That metal store on the corner was a drug store. Behind it was a hotel. What the salesmen used to do was ride the train, come in on the train, sell at the stores in Dalton, they would stay overnight and catch the train to the next town."

It's worth noting that despite it's fairly populous nature in the early 1920s, Dalton still held strong to its humble, agricultural roots. During our interviews I heard tales about the place on the hill that made sorghum molasses and the well that used to pump water up to the school. There were dirt roads lined with cattails that guarded crops of cantaloupe that you could smell as you passed by, and neighbors who raised livestock. His father was a farmer, and Grandpa himself worked at a grain elevator in his teens. This north-central Missouri town thrived in its heyday.

CHAPTER 1 - ON CHILDHOOD

This is the place where Grandpa James was raised and it shaped his life's foundation. To know this town, is to know Grandpa. For him, it is home, and a return to many fond memories.

As he recounts his stories, there's a glimmer in his eyes that shines brightly. It's unmistakeable - there is deep love for his childhood in Dalton. It's written all over his face as he tells me about his time in Phyllis Wheatley Elementary School.

> "You had to be six years old before you could go to school. School started before I was six, so I was almost 7 before I could go to school."

He continues to name a handful of his classmates from first grade; they didn't have kindergarten back then. Recalling their names brings another story to the forefront of his mind. His first year at school began with an adventure that only he can tell. Scan the code to hear more about the coat closet story in his own words (or read it below):

So Okay...

Grandpa James and The Coat Closet

"OKAY. Now my first year there. Uh, I don't know, I was probably messing up because you do, you did that. The teacher put me in the closet with the clothes, you know the clothes closet. Put me out of the classroom in there 'cause I was, I was laughing at something. A horse and wagon went down by the school. The father was old like me. He was sitting up in the wagon and his son was down on the ground, holding the horses back. So I'm looking out the window and saw it and started laughing, see. The teacher put me in the clothes closet for laughing at school.

Okay, I put on my coat and hat and stuff and when she looked up, I'm coming out. I'm going home. She run to catch me, I'm going out the door. I picked up a brick and threw it. She shut the door and it went through the panel of the door - just whomp. I went on home. I told mom and daddy about it. They took me back and they got onto the teacher about putting me in the closet. 'We didn't send a son here for you to put in the closet.' So they took up for me. I was wrong but they still took up for me. So that was the first thing that I thought I got in trouble about. From then on I was always into something, but I just went on."

This was just the start of several of Grandpa's ornery adventures but hidden in his words you'll find our first universal gem,

"From then on I was always into something, but I just went on."

Childhood is about pure joy and discovery, testing boundaries, learning, and persisting. *Grandpa and the Coat Closet*, checked off all of these childhood basics. When faced with an opportunity to dislike school because of a sour experience, he (with his parents firm guidance) chose to continue pursuing his education. As his childhood progressed, grandpa would find himself in jams of even greater proportion, learning from each experience and moving on, growing into the man that I know today. Think about the most memorable experiences from your childhood, the good ones and those you will never tell another soul about. Which childhood checklist items were covered? How do you carry that experience with you today?

Our childhoods lay a strong foundation for our adult lives. Within that lies the potential to choose your own adventure. You have the power to use it to catapult you forward into exceptional opportunities. The good, the bad, and the ugly, all provide us with lessons we can apply in future interactions.

Chapter 2
On Education

Grandpa graduated from Dalton Vocational High School in 1942. The lessons he learned while attending the "Little Tuskegee in the West" stretched beyond purely academics. He and his classmates were provided with an education that equipped them with the tools necessary to successfully navigate the world around them. Lessons ranged from math and negro history, to english and etiquette.

Scan the QR Code to listen as Grandpa James, shares more about what made Dalton Vocational High School so special.

- QR Code on next page -

Grandpa and Dalton Vocational High School

"Okay. Everybody that went through high school had to know how to do everything. We had to take, the boys had to take farming and stuff like that. We had to learn how to sew. We had to learn how to cook. We had to learn how to swim. Just, everything a person could do it was required that we would do it. And, when we would have a social on a Friday evening, the last period before they'd go home. This Friday was one dance you would do and everybody had to do that. Everybody had to learn how to do it. If it was the Charleston, you had to Charleston. If it was Jitterbug, you had to Jitterbug. Whatever it was, everybody, we had to know, here's what they had always told us, 'When you leave here, wherever you go, you'll be able to make it.' So that's the reason that I could do anything, you know whatever. We would go out, say an animal, cows or something was having calfs and stuff like that, boys and the girls and all would go. We'd all go, you had to go see and make a report on it. That's the reason when we left Dalton Vocational High School, anything that they would let you do you would be able to handle it. That was our motto."

The educators of Dalton Vocational High School took great care in instilling the importance of acquiring as much knowledge as possible. This school was meant to empower its students to achieve a successful life beyond high school and was triumphant in doing so. Dalton Vocational students were prepared to compete with the best of the best through spelling bees, state vocal music competitions, and national track meets. Each event provided an opportunity for black or as my grandfather says, "we were negro back then" students, to see each other thriving and excelling, which instilled confidence in their abilities despite what they were being sold by their white counterparts. Educators like my grandfather's favorite, Ms. Jackson, from Sedalia, MO, who taught at Dalton Vocational High School and left to join the Women's Army Corps (WAC), left a legacy of service and responsibility that resonated with their students - enough so that my grandparents sought her out on a post-WWII visit to the Missouri State Fair.

In any school, the goal is to prepare its students for life. At Dalton Vocational High School, the instructors took a page from educator John Dewey, and sought to provide hands on opportunities for its students to learn and apply relevant material, impressing upon them that education itself is life. Indeed the groundwork laid at

Dalton Vocational High School would serve as a model that grandpa would follow throughout his life. Seeking not just to increase job-based knowledge, but also his personal skills. In doing so he would find opportunities to elevate himself and his family.

After graduating from Dalton Vocational High School, Grandpa James moved to Salina, KS and soon thereafter began work building airbases around the country for a company based in Soux City, Iowa. He moved to Kansas City and married my grandmother not long after that, then faced one of their more challenging moments in life. Grandpa was drafted into the 9th Cavalry of the U.S. Army, during the height of WWII.

Following basic training and during his service, Grandpa James was promoted from a Private to a Sergeant, which he attributes to the amount of education he had received in Dalton.

> "All the tests to enter the army only went up to 6th grade. Well I could score 100 on all of those ya see!"

It was Dalton's preparation that equipped him with the skills to potentially become an officer, a path which he would decline for personal reasons. While in Italy and now assigned to the 74th Field Artillery Battalion, 22nd Cavalry, 3rd Platoon, he and two classmates from Dalton Vocational picked out places to visit based on what they read about in their history classes. He was able to see the remains of the city of Pompeii in person, along with the

Leaning Tower of Pisa, the Coliseum ruins in Rome, and the Vatican. He described the visits as if it, "was just like looking at the pictures right in front of you."

I bet right now you're interested in finding out more about his time in the service. This isn't the right chapter yet. Trust me, we'll dig deeper into his service in the Army in due time.

Following a few years of service Grandpa returned to Kansas City taking a 2-3 months break before working for a year in a Cold Storage facility in the River Market area, and then eventually beginning his career with the United States Postal Service. It was here that he would abundantly apply those lessons instilled many years ago in Dalton.

At each stage in his career with the Post Office, Grandpa James received continued training to increase his knowledge on the job. In some instances he had to be more covert in gaining this information, even going so far as to allow other training participants to believe that he was the janitor to do so.

> "I had been going to school over in Missouri. I would go over there. Nothing in there but white boys, but they thought I was the janitor there, see. I didn't do no paperwork or nothin' around them or nothin'. I'd just sit in on the things (classes) and the guy would take me afterwards and we would go over things, you know, to be sure that I had it."

It was his pursuit of knowledge and a greater understanding of what might come that pushed Grandpa James to continue "in spite of" potential barriers, people included. He knew that opportunities stay when you are well equipped to handle them. So, he continued to attend regional trainings, one of which occurred over the course of a week in Norman, Oklahoma. Here he was able to show each of his classmates the importance (and benefits) of paying attention to all the details. Take a listen as grandpa tells us about this training and its final exam.

Grandpa and The Final Exam

"I went to school in Norman, Oklahoma for the post-office. Okay, the machines that we had to handle the mail, ordinarily everything goes this way, go right. So we had to go up and different ones were showing how the mail would go through and flip it over and this and that and the other and everything, and they would go the right way, see. So I went up there and I went the other way! So the guy that was in charge says, 'Robinson go back and show him why you went the wrong way.' I says, 'since I was the only black one in the class, I just wanted to be different!' That's what I told him see. Ha, ha ha! So he said, 'No, take this pointer and go back there and show them why you did it.' and I went up there and showed them that lil' ole thing in the corner where it was.

But you see, in a school they put those tricks in there you see. And so, okay...you had to take a final examination when you finished. We were down there a whole week. So I'm back there and so he was sitting back there and talking. I says, 'will you quit talking to me so I can write something?' He says, 'I correct the papers!' I said, 'oh okay, let's talk.' I had nothin on my paper and I made the highest grade in the whole class! It was boys in there from the east and from the west, you know. From post offices all around. I made the highest score of all. He says, 'that one deal let me know that you know what to do'. And if you read, it don't make no difference what you got, there's something on there that'll tell you what to do... and if you get to something, look at it first and read it."

There are often great advantages that accompany a complete education, and every now and then you'll find some hiccups along the way. Such is life. What Grandpa knew to be true about the value of knowledge and education (formal or informal) is also something that I have heard regularly growing up, and have shared with countless students. It's something he lived and passed on through his example.

> *"If you're educated, you can hold your own anywhere."*

And he did.

Chapter 3
On Work & Discipline

You might remember from earlier that Grandpa James worked in a grain elevator. In high school he would test the eggs & butterfat, and also transported coal, working for 35 cents/hr. When he wasn't working at the elevator he would have an opportunity to make a bit of money on the side. "That's not unusual," I thought to myself as he told me this. What I didn't see coming though was Grandpa James, the Frugal Horseman. Listen along as he tells you how to save some money!

Grandpa James the Frugal Horseman

> "There's one man there, had a horse that had to run. His
> name was Holland Bayne, and the horse's name was Fred.
> He would walk the horse to town, he lived out on a farm.
> Find me, give me 15 cents for my lunch, and the horse
> and I would take off running. We would run from Dalton
> to Glasgow, which is 20 miles or so and I would eat
> dinner with my grandparents. They lived in Glasgow, see.
> Save that 15 cents! And, we were known, that when they
> see us going, the farmers going by the farmers, 'There
> go James and Fred'. They knew us. He was a horse that I
> could walk, he would be in the pasture, and I'd walk out
> to the fence and he would come to the fence like a dog
> would. You know, just come to see me. He figured we
> was gon' get a chance to run. I mean just quit what he was
> doing and come to the fence where I could rub his head
> and whatnot."

Through this story, Grandpa shared two patterns that persisted
throughout his career; 1) the importance of saving where you
can, and 2) just how far your treatment of others will stretch.

Although Fred was a horse, had my grandpa treated him with
disrespect, he most certainly would not have met him at the fence
when he saw him. In fact, he would have been more difficult to
ride each time Mr. Bayne brought him into town.

More than likely, Mr. Bayne would have noticed Fred's hesitancy and found a new horseman to run him. See, customer service is just as valuable today as it was when my grandfather was running Fred, which he did until just after high school when moved from Dalton, MO. In the years that would follow, any return visit to see family in Dalton, yielded a visit to Fred's pasture. Fred would always come to the fence to greet Grandpa James, hoping for another opportunity to run. When you treat someone well, they remember.

After grandpa graduated from Dalton Vocational High School, his brother LeRoy got an offer to help a contractor build airbases for 90 cents/hr. Well that offer was too good to pass up.

> "It was time and a half after 8 hours, double time on Saturdays and Sundays. Woooo! That was much money! God I tell ya," grandpa shared.

Sure, much money could motivate you, but your work ethic must also be solid to last through such taxing work, day in and day out. He considered continuing with that contractor but chose instead to move to Kansas City, where he was soon drafted into the Army. Still not that chapter. It's coming though. I promise.

Most of Grandpa's co-workers from the Post-Office would mirror the same affinity for him as Fred the Horse. He spent 42 years building his skills, developing relationships, and working to ensure that the Post Office functioned smoothly enough to provide quality service to its customers from the inside out. His work ethic was second to none, using less than a handful of sick days in total throughout nearly 5 decades of employment. He was dedicated to the work and ensuring things were right across the board.

Grandpa James visit the Post Office in Washington, D.C.

He once encountered a location in Northeast Kansas without a restroom. Hear how it got resolved.

Grandpa James and the Toilet

"And here again, it was one of those deals that, because I had been around people, that, it didn't, they didn't excite me. You know what I mean? Yeah, they was just another person, you know. I didn't pay no attention to em. Yeah. One woman up there said, 'Where you going from here Mr. Robinson?' I says, 'I'm going to such-an-such-a place.' 'Well you better use my toilet cause she don't have a toilet.' I say, 'A post office without a toilet?' She say, 'Yeah, she don't have one.' I called the district manager, I didn't call my boss. I called over him and I told him. He says, 'There's no running water.' I says, 'Well it's a big water tower across the street here!' And I says, 'it's water in the building but it's no fixtures, no stool or nothin', no hand, nothin', you know, nothin' in the…the room is there and nothin's in it! And she's been there 12 years!' He says, 'you go over there and take her with you, take the Postmaster with you so they'll know, 'cause, you know, they don't know you up there. And tell them that you want them to, tell them what you want 'em to do, and put it in writing, and then when they get it done, then they call you, say - we don't want no price, we just want you to do it - and when you get it done, I'll be back and inspect it, and I'll get your money.' Oh man, and everybody in the north and the east end of Kansas knew, Mr. Robinson got so-in-so, I can't think of her name, got her a toilet. Yeah, Mr. Robinson did this."

The toilet was just one of many instances where Grandpa James would right a wrong. His job was to see to it that things ran smoothly within each post office, but his passion was in ensuring things were equitable from branch to branch. Sure this Post Office functions well, but lack of facilities doesn't just equal a loss in productivity. It's also a loss of human dignity. The same holds true for a sticking door.

Get your QR scanner ready to listen to another Grandpa James original story.

- QR Code on next page -

Grandpa James and the Metal Door

"They put in a metal door, frame and all, and he couldn't get the door to close. With the shutter on it, it wouldn't close. And he, the guy that bid on the job was from Oklahoma. He'd gone back to Oklahoma. I told the engineer, I says, 'The door's not right.' He says, 'Well that's the best he could do.' I said, 'Well did you pay him?' 'Yeah, yeah.' Okay. So I took a guy, one of my mechanics. I had been for 2-3 years trying to get him to be a mechanic, so I could teach him what to do. He didn't want to be one. He was just wanting to be a janitor and that's all. That was a level 3 or 4 or something like that. Well if he'd have been a mechanic, he'd have been a level 6. So finally, I got hold to his wife and I told her about it, and she didn't know that I had been trying to do that. So she made him come on in, see. So I said, 'Well okay.' I took him with me. I took a wooden block and a sledge hammer, and I gave him some tools, issued him some tools and everything. I says now, 'I want you to, around this door, where them bolts come through, loosen them up just a little bit. All the way around.' I say I put that wooden block in that corner, then take that thing and BOOM! The door says, KADUNK. I say, 'Now tighten it up.' I said, 'but don't you tell nobody what happened.' I said 'Don't EVER mention it! Don't ever mention it 'cause the things I'm telling you, they're between you and I.' I didn't hit it but one time! And that man was a contractor, was supposed to have been, sheee, he wouldn't, he couldn't, he'd gone on back to Oklahoma. He couldn't get it to close. It would hang on him, see. Sheee, I put that thing in that corner and hit that thing. And that metal door stretched out or whatever. We locked it back up and it's working today! Yeah, it's still working."

If not fixed it might slow down staff, but would the same sticking door be allowed elsewhere? So, with Grandpa James in charge, it gets fixed in Turner and anywhere else it might occur. That is the equitable and just way to approach work. To do something right the first time, should always be the goal. If by chance that doesn't work, follow up until the job is done right.

He had a history of being knowledgable on the job. Grandpa's funny bone was tickled when telling me about a time when his knowledge wasn't trusted by a new supervisor. Quite frankly, mine was tickled too. The story involved a backed up toilet and, well, you'll just have to hear how Grandpa got things resolved.

- QR Code follows -

A headshot from Grandpa's days at the Post Office

Grandpa James and 250 Twice Over

"The lines in the womens' toilet, they would put stuff in their and choke it. I ordered one of them. That ole proctor, hadn't been here very long see. And so, he told her see, 'Find out from Robinson, do he need this?' And so she come back, said, 'The Postmaster said do you need this?' I didn't say nothin' for a while. Then I told her, I says, 'naw, I don't need it.' Just like that. So, she went back and told him, 'He said no he didn't need it. But I didn't like that look on his face.' So he called down for me to come. I went up to his office. He said, 'Well she said that you didn't look so well when I asked about this.' I said, 'Well' I says uhh, ' it stops up and...' 'Ain't it some other way you can do it?' I says, 'Oh yes, there's plenty of ways to do it.' 'We gonna do it another way.'

The thing cost less than $150. So, I called Roto Rooter. 250! I told him, 'Don't, don't give me no bill. Wait 'til the end of the month.' Called him twice. Five hundred dollars! When he got that bill for $500 he called me. He said, 'What's this?' I said, 'That's that other way that you told me to do it.' I says, I says, 'Now whaddya, whaddya want me to do? Go down in there and crawl down in there myself and get it out?' I said, 'Naw, naw, naw, naw! You told me to do something else and that's just what I did.' He said, 'I ain't gon' never question you about nothin' no more!' I says, 'I don't, I'm not here to just buy stuff just for the thing!' I says, 'If I don't need it, I ain't gon' buy it!' And he didn't. Hee hee hee hee. Yeah!"

Through his actions, Grandpa James delivered a lesson about trusting people to do their job. It is a lesson that stuck with this supervisor for years. He shared it with others in hopes that they too would grow to understand that,

"if you take away someone's ability to do their job, it will cost you."

Chapter 4
On Challenge & Errors

Challenge found its way to Grandpa pretty regularly. Most often off the court. In high school though, it came in the form of a State Championship basketball game. Dalton Vocational High School was outmatched and a clear underdog. I'll let him tell you more about how he and his team handled the challenge. Scan the code to hear the story he almost forgot to share.

So Okay...

Grandpa James and the Championship Game

"I did tell you about us playing basketball for the championship."

"Ummm, ummm."

"Aww God, well, we played, we played, Sumner of, of, of, Sumner of St. Louis for the championship for the state of Missouri of basketball - for the championship. Now we, Dalton Vocational High School was B, and this one was A. Now the number of people in your school, your school was A and B. And at the end of the year we met, and whoever would finish was the champion of the state. OKAY, I'm the center. So you know what size team we had. I'm the tallest one in the bunch. So the coach put me in. You couldn't talk to them. You had to pull them out, stop the thing and pull 'em out and talk to 'em and whatnot. So the coach told me, 'James,' and this team was givin' us, all them boys was tall and big. He says, 'Go and shoot your shots from the center." That's where I used to shoot from all the time. I would have to shoot so many of them before I could leave the court at home. So that's where, see, they're not gonna come out there in the center ways. Just as you get over the center shoot it. Okay, they made a basket and we come back down and I got ready to shoot and Bubba (his cousin) squealed. He had a sound, a different sound than anybody. Bubba was wide open under the basket! Look, I did the (imitates a sky hook pass) to Bubba and it rolled off. The crowd, I said I'd lost it then and I turned and run back. The crowd hollered. I didn't know what the dickens was going on. So when them guys they came back down with one. And so I asked Bubba, I said, 'Bubba, what happened?' He said, 'It went in the basket!' I said, 'It did?' He said, 'Yeah! Yeah, man!' So we come down, I hit my spot and I shot it that time. I made it, Boom! Just like that, see. I said, 'Okay.' They made one. I came back down then got it and just as I got ready to shoot, look - I could see two of them guys comin' in here. Yeah. I let the ball go and fell and they heads hit, and the heads rattled you know. Have you ever heard people's heads rattle? That head rattled, just 'BGLURGLUR'! Just like that. They had to take both of 'em off the court. We won the championship that year. Yeah, shoot yes. We won the championship that year. But that was two of they best men was, they was fixinta wipe me out see."

Through an errant pass, Grandpa was able find the basket. Lucky shot, maybe. But success in an unconventional method worked out for the best and led to favorable results. Their team found consistently unorthodox ways to outplay their overmatched opponent. The error did not define their outcome. They determined it for themselves.

As you might be able to tell from this story and those about the

Hog, the Coat Closet, and 250 Twice Over, Grandpa is a bit of a character. I have yet to tell you about the time he beat his hat for running away, and that said hat was on someone's head during said beating. In his own words, when he was younger, he "was a booger." There were ornery occasions that he produced, as well as times when challenge was brought to him. Perhaps the greatest of these occurred upon his abrupt discharge from the Army.

The war was over and his unit was now stateside. Listen as Grandpa tells you more about their rushed exit from Jefferson Barracks in St. Louis, Missouri.

Grandpa James and the Jefferson Barracks

"Okay, we was at the Jefferson Barracks in St. Louis getting out. And the ole Recruiting Sergeant says, 'Anybody that wants to re-enlist I'm gon' put you at the head of the line. So you can go home on a vacation and come back.' And we didn't let him do that, see. So, they had a scuffle there about that and one guy from Jefferson City pulled out a knife about 6" long and then opened the blade on it. See so that looked like a corn knife. That booger, the Recruiting Sergeant took out the back door running. And this dude was running at him, cutting at him, see. So we, we trashed the place. While he was running him, we threw the furniture through the closed down windows and stuff. And so, they sent us outta there, and a downtown to get the train. I couldn't, they wouldn't let us go in the station. We had to sit outside and wait 'til the train come. But what it did, it got me home one day before my wife's birthday. If it hadn't been for that, I never would've made it on her birthday. So I made it home. I got out one day, outta there. And my, the only thing on my discharge that I put down, was honorable. The rest of it is what they wanna put on there. Nothin' bout the 117 Cavalry, Buffalo Cavalry, stuff like that. It wasn't none of that. It was 9th and 10th. It wasn't no 117 nothin'. That's what's on my, that's what's on my thing. I said, it didn't make no difference, I didn't, I didn't care. I was just outta there. Yeah 'cause see, they made me go in, and I got out!"

Grandpa's departure was so quick that his discharge papers don't reflect accurate information from his time in the service. Missing from the document are his tour in World War II, and appointment to the 9th Cavalry. Though, they would have been distinct honors to have included on your discharge papers, the priority for Grandpa was to have an honorable discharge. That afforded him an unexpected bonus, the opportunity to arrive home just in time for his wife's birthday in a fashion reminiscent of a scene from a movie.

> As he told me, "It was like a blizzard. The snow was comin' all around us. It was piled so high the cab driver couldn't make it all the way up the street. So I told him it was far enough and I could make it the rest of the way. I had to walk through the snow to get there but I made it just in time for her birthday!"

For his family's sake, his discharge from the Army marked the start of their expansion; from a family of three to a family of four and beyond, until eight children and two parents inhabited their home. Lemons, meet Lemonade.

Neither challenge nor error should define your existence. Though their arrival is hardly pleasing, they provide a favorable time to course correct and find a new path towards your desired results. Without our own challenges and errors, we wouldn't be who we are today. They help to strengthen our resolve and rattle our heads enough to temporarily shake up our routine. To combat them you must know what you value and be prepared to shoot your shot, the one you practice all the time.

Chapter 5
On Courage

I alluded to Grandpa's tenacity in the Introduction of this book. To say he's experienced a myriad of opportunities to demonstrate his courage might just be the understatement of all understatements. Anyone who has lived 94 years on this earth has had their character tested several times over.

Imagine though, the journey of a man whose own grandmother was born a slave. I'll rephrase this so you can envision it in your own life. Imagine how different your journey would be if your grandmother was born into slavery. What lessons would you learn from her life? What challenges would the two of you face together in the post-slavery era? What we're talking about is a man who himself was born in the middle of the Jim Crow era of United States history. Envision the blatant racism that attempted to gobble up and swallow his existence on every level; within his workplace, at home, in his community, while attempting to raise a thriving family.

The truly unfortunate side of withstanding "separate but equal" practices that upheld the perpetuation of segregation, of being on the receiving end of hurled rocks and racial slurs, is that each human being who received this treatment at the hands of another had to wrestle with feeling as though it was their problem to fix. In actuality, this problem was the offspring of sheer ignorance and fear. It was raised by those who desired to control and manipulate others into assimilation and was abandoned in someone else's neighborhood, suddenly thrust upon others to deal with. Not only did ethnic minorities not ask for any of the received treatment, but they were also now faced with having to make sense of an utterly ridiculous and ever moving target of living an acceptable existence in the eyes of someone who had no desire to share "their world". It is enough to suffocate the soul if not for receiving consistent community support and using each negative to strengthen their resolve to create a place that is better for their children. The strength and true grit that developed in the face of pain, grief, and trauma became a living, breathing example of courage for generations to come. Through his trials, Grandpa was able to sharpen his saw across dimensions; each act refining the blades which yielded faster, cleaner cuts as time progressed.

His saw began to sharpen very early in life. During our conversations, Grandpa wouldn't share what he viewed when he was younger, only shaking his head at the tough experiences he'd lived through and witnessed, and offering the words, "Your grandfather's been through hell and high water!" He did, however, speak of his time in high school; traveling to other schools for athletics events. The tone of his voice shifted when discussing each unsolicited experience of discrimination. One of the earliest memories shared was from his days of playing high school basketball.

Grandpa James and his teammates took a trip to Salina, KS for a basketball game. When they arrived they were told they would be unable to play because they were negro. They weren't even allowed to deboard the bus at the high school. He told us about a feeling that sat in the pit of their stomachs and the anger that rose but could not escape.

The ride back to Dalton, MO in deafening silence gave each student a chance to sift through their anger, and refocus their energy into an ability to do something different next time. That opportunity would be there before they knew it.

SO OKAY...

Grandpa James and the Rock Slingers

"We would play wherever we went or whatever we did,
they umm, they wold want to run us out of town. A bus
driver, had graduated from high school and he was driving
the school bus. He decided we would go on the railroad
tracks and pick up some rocks and get us a bucket of
rocks, and take it with us. We took 'em to Chillicothe.
The game was over and then they started rockin' us out
of town. We started throwing the rocks back in the dark,
see. They wondered how in the world we could find
rocks in the dark! Well, we said that was the rocks they
threw at us. So we broke the windows out of the school
and everything else. Yeah, we broke windows out of the
school and everything, but we won the game. But, the
word got around that we could see rocks in the dark, so it
never did happen anymore."

Protection was a necessity but the rocks hurled in return served
as much more. Each rock thrown at the aggressors sharpened the
saw of each Dalton Vocational High School student on the bus.
With each throw, regardless of the impact, each young man was
increasing his resilience and fight. This would be greatly needed
as the world entered into a battle which would pluck many young
men from their families, placing them in conditions that would
test their physical, mental, and emotional fortitude. Indeed their
strength to continue would be more of a necessity than anyone
could have predicted.

Enter World War II. Grandpa James, part of a Field Artillery Battalion, found himself still linked to challenges similar to those he could find at home in the United States.

Grandpa James in Italy, Part I

"Okay, here we go into Pompeii. So, I'm driving the truck 'cause it was on a Sunday or some time. It must've been on a Sunday 'cause we was down in Naples. And we went downtown, going through the town. The Provost Marshals, they was white. They looked out and saw some black soldiers on the thing. They jumped in their little Ford car and started after us, see. Said we was speedin'. The highways over there is narrow, so I got in the middle of it and they couldn't get by us. They had red lights on us and everything. Everybody on the trucks turned their backs to 'em, see. We got out of that over into the British Zone. That's when I stopped. Well they can't bring me back now, see. They can't bring me back. So, they made a report to my captain and they recommend taking my driver's license 'way from me. So I said, 'that didn't make no difference no way,' 'cause most of the time my jeep driver always drove for me anyway. So okay, we went to Pompeii. Visited the city. They had stuff that you could see in there."

Through each experience Grandpa had the audacity to stand dauntless in the face of each asinine aggressor in pursuit of a greater truth; equal treatment as a human being. His Corporal found out about the driver's license confiscation when another team of drivers was lax in their ability to deliver their cargo in a timely manner, taking more than twice as long as it should have taken. When in search of a man who could do the job right, the Corporal was informed about Grandpa James who could do it but recently had his license revoked. As the story goes, the corporal raised a fuss with anyone within earshot. Eventually Grandpa was tasked with the job and followed through on his responsibilities, just as the Corporal had been promised.

Grandpa James in Italy, Part II

"So okay, we went and left there. He got put on the truck, the four trucks. But the boxes was no more than, a little bigger than my t (the tv stand) but it had ropes in the end of it see. We don't know what was in 'em. So, I was supposed to go to between, see from where we were to Rome was 500 miles. So, halfway there they were supposed to have somebody to meet me, and we was to come back. Well we got there and wasn't nobody there. They gassed up our trucks and everything, and gave us something to eat and stuff and said, 'Go again!' We got to Rome. Same thing at Rome. So, I said, 'I wonder what in the world is happening here.' So we left there and went to Bari. That's in, Bari's in sight of Switzerland. You can look over and, you know Kansas City, KS and Kansas City, MO? Yeah, yeah, yeah, yeah, see. But I didn't go over there. So okay, we went on up there, and when we got there, the guns was shooting over the top of us. The big guns! And we got to the place where we was supposed to go and a private first class, no generals, no colonels, no nothin' was there. Only enlisted men was there. He had some men and each one of them took an end of that box and took off with 'em on foot. Yeah."

There they were. Thousands of miles from their respective homes. Working together towards one common goal. The saw continued to sharpen for black soldiers and the Second World War offered a new perspective for the white soldiers who served along side them.

Upon their return from World War II, black and white soldiers alike reached within to pull from the determination and strength they used to fight the enemy abroad. The need this time was to fight the enemy on American soil. They had supported and protected each other through the most challenging times, each helping the other to return home to their loved ones. Then stood courageously united in the face of social injustice and pushing for change in the form of equitable civil liberties.

Often we ask why we alone should be the courageous one. Well, sometimes that strength is more powerful in numbers. As my grandfather referenced, the fight for equality gained traction when they got a bit more help.

Grandpa James and the Fight to End Segregation

"Well, we were still segregated. And when we came out

of the service we made up our mind then that we was gon'
end that segregation. See because, the soldiers that was,
the white boys that was with us when we was in service, it
wasn't, we had to stick together and watch out for each
other. And we had enough of them had been around us
to know, and to be able to try to help us to do what has to
be done."

Courage comes in many forms but it is ultimately a pursuit,

"...to do what has to be done."

Each day we all have the opportunity to sharpen our saw, increasing
our fortitude and spirit for the good of humankind. It is far easier
to cower in the face of challenge and avoid confrontation, but
the results of daring to change things within our circles (home,
community, country, etc.) far surpass what any of us can imagine.
To be not deterred by confrontations from the agitated serves only
to empower others to do the same. It is a ripple effect for good
that will spread far and wide beyond our sight. The absolute truth
is that we all possess the power to make more of an impact than we
know. When our displays of fearlessness breed an environment
for others' courage to blossom and bloom, the pattern repeats
itself for all who witness the new flourish of flowers.

Chapter 6
On Family

Grandpa James was named after his uncle James Monroe Basey, one of his mom's many older brothers. By my accounts there were 13 Basey siblings born of William & Lucy, Grandpa's grandparents. Grandpa James' mom and dad raised 12 children together. Grandpa James and Grandma Liz raised 8 children, so large families are not uncommon to find in our family tree. Listen as Grandpa recalls how his family grew so large.

Grandpa James and The Growing Family

> "As a youngster you didn't know nothin'. You would go
> where you got to to stay all night down to Aunt Bessie
> or Uncle Pete's or something like that. We'd stay all
> night down there and come back home we had a brother
> or sister or something like that. We was almost grown
> before we found out what was going on!"

As he would share some of the stories about my distant relatives, I
would jot down a name or two along with some details about how
we were connected in hopes of later finding them in the family
tree. As I began to piece together the quilt of our family story I
found myself in awe as the Aunt Bessie's and Uncle Pete's were
revealed. Because of grandpa's stories I somehow felt like I knew
each person as I would find them.

My 2nd great-grandpa Basey, who lived in Glasgow, Missouri,
my 3rd great-grandpa McAdams, I got to know their character
through the lens of Grandpa James. There were stories that were
passed on to him through a combination of his own personal
experience, and family anecdotes that were handed down through
the years from griot to griot. I'll never know if they planned for
each story to travel as far as this but I'm grateful for the gift of
family connection. I had not realized it was missing until it was
suddenly present. It's sort of like that sweater you bought during
an end of season sale and tucked away to wear when it's cold again.
In the recesses of my mind I knew there was a deep family history

Grandpa's Parents: Verland & Minnie Robinson

but I didn't realize just how much I longed to know its details until it revealed itself. Much like the excitement and confidence you feel in rediscovering that yet to be worn sweater when the temperature drops again, learning about your roots and your family history lights a fire that yields an air of certainty and purpose-driven poise.

In thinking about the words of Robert Louis Stevenson, "Every heart that has beat strongly and cheerfully has left a hopeful impulse behind it in the world, and bettered the tradition of mankind." I am reminded that the more connected you are to your family, the stronger your heartbeat. The stronger your heartbeat, the more hopeful your outlook on what can be done. This is a stronghold of Grandpa James' existence, a strong pulse connected to his family and great hope for better days ahead.

He smiled during each interview as he recanted his family experience, both with immediate siblings and his children alike. Being born in the middle of the pack of 12, he had the opportunity to get to know most of his siblings, those older and younger than him. There was always someone to help out and it was not uncommon that his family would jump in to do so. He described a time that he watched his brother Boyd as he attempted to help their neighbor with car problems. Take a listen.

- QR Code on next page -

Grandpa James and his Siblings

Grandpa James and The Chandler Handler

"Mr. Sam Lewis worked on the railroad and he lived across the street. It was a house, where our house is here, it was a house over here, and a fence around it and he had a Chandler. he had a Chandler. That's a BIG car! So, Mamie, his daughter, came out one day, backed it out in the yard, and come out the gate and said, 'Come on Boyd and go with me!' She couldn't stop it and he couldn't catch up with her, and she went on. So Boyd run down the block and he couldn't catch her. So he come on back. So Mamie came on back, running about 5 - 10 miles an hour and went back in the yard, went in the garage, then went on through the garage out into the garden. It was a nice garage! You know back in those days the lumber was pine lumber, you know good, good stuff. You get anything now. No, no it was good! Mamie went on out in the garden. That's when it stopped. So Boyd told her, 'Well Mamie, why didn't you tell me and we could've started it. I could've been with you to start with!' She said, 'well I thought I could handle it.'"

I'd like to think it was his brother's willingness to help that stood out most to grandpa James. Maybe it was the waste of good lumber that he remembers most. But what I found in this story was a sense of community that was fostered within their household of 6 boys and 6 girls all working together to help things run as efficiently as possible. My great uncle Boyd's desire to help was not a rare sight. In fact this was reflective of the importance of family. The prominence of the value of family in their lives laid a foundation for many actions yet to follow, including Grandpa James' request to see his 6 month old first-born child prior to spending 21 days on the water as he headed out for the war.

Listen and read along as grandpa recants his request for a short reprieve to see his newborn son.

Grandpa James and Baby Jim

"So, I asked the captain, see Jim, my oldest, Jim was born then see and I hadn't ever seen him. So I asked the captain if it would be possible that I could go home and see my son. He said well let me go to the battalion headquarters and see what I can do. and he went to the colonel and the colonel run him out of the office. And the reason I know what happened, a friend of mine was a clerk in the office, McGaughy was his name - he's from North Carolina, but he was in the office see. And so, 45 minutes, he come back again! And he says, 'What kinda man are we talking about to have you back here again?' So, he looked at him (McGaughy) and he started putting in words. He said, 'Aww shut up McGaughy and get this man outta here!' They let me come home and when I went back, I had to catch up with them in Newport News, Virginia. Yeah! They let me come home to see Jim. I never had seen him."

Seeing his son was a miracle that almost didn't happen had it not been for an officer who also saw the importance of family. That quick trip home nearly solidified grandpa's return to Kansas City. It was the thought of returning home to his wife and new son that Grandpa James held tight to during tough times. Further strengthening his resolve to return home came in the form of a happenstance visit to his cousin Bubba, whom he surprised during the middle of the war.

Grandpa James and Bubba's Awakening

"We got them trucks and everything, and on our way from there I saw a supply truck for food for an outfit and it had the numbers on the truck that a cousin of mine was there. So, we followed him on in. You know where he went on in under the what do you call that stuff, the shelter, the camouflage. Went on in under the camouflage, and I told the first sergeant, I says 'I got a cousin out here in your outfit, his name's James Blackwell,' and she says 'He's out here in the sleep cause he was out last night and he's in the sleep.' Says, 'Go out there and wake him up. Go wake him up. I know he would love to see you!' So I went out there.

At home, in Dalton we called him Bubba. So I went out there and shook him and I said, 'Bubba! Bubba!' He opened his eyes and looked at me and shut em back up. I said, 'Bubba! Bubba!' and it come to him what had happened and Lord he jumped up and grabbed me and we hugged and went on! In there, they didn't use that nickname. He hadn't heard that Bubba since he left Dalton, see. That was two years or better. Almost three years! He hadn't heard Bubba. Oh Lord! So, we went and talked with the ole First Sergeant and we stayed there overnight. And like my captain told me, you just take your time and come back. We came back to Rome and ole Mussolini's place where he had, they had taken it over. Rest camp, we stayed there. Then we came on back to Naples. But oh buddy, they was....it was, it was something!"

Bubba's First Sergeant was intuitively aware of the value of one man seeing his family, and understood the residual effects it would have on the soul of his entire unit. It likens back to the Stevenson quote, when one man has hope it spreads like a ripple to those around him. And that's the impact of nurturing a solid relationship with family.

While that left a lasting impact on Grandpa James, Bubba, and Bubba's unit, there still lingered thoughts of hometown friends who weren't as lucky to return home after World War II. This left grandpa with an opportunity to extend support to his Dalton family, especially the parents of soldiers who would not be coming home.

He cried with the family of Purple Heart recipient, Sergeant

Sydnor Webb, whose last breath fell during turmoil in Italy. "You have to support each other in good times as well as the tough times," he shared with me during our final interview. And when it's you, who's facing the tough times, be okay with receiving help. Remember,

"you don't know everything...even the President has helpers."

Indeed that's what family is all about. Lifting each other as you decipher how to climb is an essential part of growing together. Life's journey is far easier to navigate with the support of your family, both those who were chosen for you and those you chose along the way. Be they large in number or small and mighty, maintaining a connection with your family can strengthen the beat of your heart and leave a trail of hope for others to follow.

Chapter 7
On Connection

I haven't mentioned it yet but Grandpa James was a man of many trades. While he worked at the Post Office during the day, he was also moonlighting as a television deliveryman for Western Auto during the evenings and weekends, driving a truck for another business owner. Despite Grandpa's ability to drive and deliver, things didn't pan out as planned for that owner. However, the televisions still needed delivering.

Dave Durham, of Western Auto reached out to Grandpa for help. Scan the code and listen to Grandpa tell the story about how Robinson's Delivery service came to be.

- QR Code on next page -

Grandpa James and the Start of Robinson's Delivery

"So, Dave Durham told me, says 'You got a truck?' I says, 'Yeah I got a truck, but my Daddy's got it down in Dalton.' He says, 'Well, go down to Fells Chevrolet and tell 'em. I'll call down there and tell 'em let you have a truck.' And that's how I started what I had. And he was the man who named it Robinson's Delivery. Yeah, yeah. And that's where we started."

One man and his truck soon became one man, his sons and a truck. Over the course of many years of steady business, Robinson's Delivery Service grew into one man, his kids, staff, and many trucks. Lots of people have a truck and a desire to start something. How though, did it grow? It took a solid connection with people.

I'm sure you've heard the phrase, "it's not what you know but who

Son #2 and a truck

you know." I tend to think that a strong combination of the two yields different results than purely possessing just one. I could know someone who has an in at the best company in the world for building robust glomtoms, but unless I know something about glomtoms, I'd have a hard time lasting in the company - in any position. As an aside, I don't think glomtoms are an actual thing, but you could substitute any item in its place and the truth would remain. You must have a fundamental working knowledge of the area in order for any of your connections to feel confident in recommending you or your services/abilities.

Grandpa had developed a strong combination of the two and that was reflected in the referrals he received. They knew his work ethic and that of his sons, his desire to do the job right, and his timeliness would all work together to complete the task just how it needed to be done.

They were asked to deliver to the homes of wealthy Kansas Citians, like the Kauffman's. But regardless of the amount of wealth the client had acquired, Grandpa treated them all the same.

Listen to Grandpa tell us more about the new refrigerator.

Grandpa James and the New Refrigerator

"Okay. We made a delivery out there to the people that used to own the ball club here. The baseball club, Kauffman, yeah. We delivered a refrigerator out there. They were down south somewhere, on vacation or something. And the one they had there in the kitchen that matches everything it quit workin'. So, the lady that lived there, she called and they told him to get another one. So he called the president of Western Auto, so they sent us out there with a nice one. And I got there, and all the thing was, it's just been settin' so long it done got dirt up in it and wasn't coolin' see. So she say, 'You gon' take, you can take it with you.' I says, 'Naw.' I say, 'We don't want to take it with us.' I says, 'Since it's no cars in there, I'mma clean it out and set it in the garage and plug it back in.' And that booger come right back on see. So okay, so she done had the woman down there done paid us extra for just coming out there see. And there, I done saved the refrigerator, and my God. I thought she thought I was the smartest man in the world! I think I ended up with something like a thousand dollars in the whole thing all together. And we went back after we let it sit out there for a week and it did what it was supposed to do. We went back and put it back in for them and everything and that's where I got the thousand, yeah. I never did see them, the only thing I saw was the maid. That's right, I never did see them."

It was his nature to provide the best service regardless of financial status that continued to bring in business. They made deliveries to homes where they had to fend off dogs, or occupants who weren't expecting deliveries. But regardless of the home, the service was the same; as exceptional as possible.

The work came in like a flood and soon they were receiving more money than was acceptable to some. You have to remember the time period in which he was working. While he did have the support of some, oftentimes Caucasian citizens objected to Negro citizens earning more than "their share". According to Grandpa, my uncle and his cousin in just one week earned around $8000. Which raised a complaint.

Grandpa and the High Dollar Help

"Made $8000. Terry and Keith, one week. Back in those days $8000 was a lot. I don't mean the rest of the, we, they just made that much themselves. And the guy, he decided that was in charge, he was gon' get somebody else. That's too much money for us to make."

In a time when America's black citizens were supposed to remain subordinate, Grandpa and his delivery service were faced with a fate that was ultimately out of his hands. Fortunately for all who have had the opportunity to work at Robinson's Delivery, there were others in position to recognize the power of numbers. One such individual told Grandpa, "Well if you made $8, we made $80!" before finding a way to right what was clearly wrong.

According to Grandpa, "if you do what you're supposed to do, it's not gonna go easy all the time...you can always get help."

The President of the company found a way to make it right because of Grandpa James' history of service and the relationship he had worked to build over the years. The time and energy you invest in others gets returned to you tenfold. His ability and desire to continually do so was returned to him more times than not and those benefits rippled into other areas of his life, including his 9-to-5.

While delivering on behalf of Robinson's Delivery, Grandpa connected with a gentleman that happened to know his supervisor at the Post Office. Because of the service he provided to this client, Grandpa unwittingly created a connection that yielded a solid recommendation for a promotion at the Post Office.

There is a repeated theme in relationship building. Our world is completely interconnected and the way you treat others can have a profound impact on future opportunities. You'll find that connecting with others adds wealth to your life far more valuable than money. You never know what people know, and who they're willing to connect you with.

Someone who Grandpa met in the Post Office possessed a miracle spray that could rid the bathroom of the smell of a million dumps. He recommended this guy's expertise to a lady they made a delivery to. She needed to rid her house of the smell of smoke after a fire. In turn, the same man connected Grandpa James with a delivery business owner who was going out of business and needed to sell his trucks.

Scan the code below to listen as Grandpa tells us all about the Mattress Man.

Grandpa James and the Mattress Man

> "Bill Schribler, he lived in Independence, and I was talkin', he was talkin' to me, and he says, he asked me he says if I 'could use some trucks'. He said, 'because they don't want to give me nothin much for 'em. And if you can use em, I'll sell them to you for what you want to give me for them.' I says, 'I can't use 'em.' I said, 'but I'll tell

you what, I'll talk to Mr. Reese where I park mine, see if we can't bring 'em over here, and, and, park 'em in his lot, and then sell 'em. And so it did, I asked Mr. Reese 'bout it and he says, 'Yep, bring em on.' We brought em over and put em in the lot. And he didn't have to rush to sell. He got a good price out of 'em. So after then, everything that would come up after he quit, everything that people that knew him as a delivery would call me and I'd go do it see. And so we uh, well, I'll tell you this, I think I told you about this man with this sprayin' thing, gets odor. He was the one that hooked me with them see. Okay, but then, we umm, after he finally sold them and everything but he was the shipping clerk at Sealy Mattress Company. And so, we went down to get some mattresses and what not, and I went with him that day. And uh, he would, the man, the owner Mr. Dodd or somebody, he was Jewish, he came out, and he told him, 'Mr. Dodd, I want you to meet Mr. Robinson here, Robinson's Delivery.' He looked at me, says, 'Bill, you didn't tell me he was a colored man!' So Bill says, 'Well I didn't have to tell you all of that. All you wanted was..' He says, 'Aww, yes. If you'd have told me that...come on in the office! I want to talk to you.' And he took me in the office, and then he and I talked. And he hooked me up with all the mattress companies all over town, Sealy's and Serta's, and everybody!"

His connection to the Funk Remover led to an opportunity to expand Robinson's Delivery Service. Grandpa credits his success

A truck from the early days of Robinson's Delivery

to a firm understanding of people and treating everyone the same no matter what. As a result, Robinson's Delivery flourished for more than 64 years.

Grandpa believes wholeheartedly that,

> *"You got to be able to understand people in order to make it."*

Indeed it was his understanding of people and what drives them that afforded Grandpa to make impactful connections that helped him successfully navigate through the start of a business and life in general.

Chapter 8
On What's Important (Love+)

On a crisp fall night as a thunderstorm marched towards the city, Grandpa and I had the chance to chat about what's important in life. I call it "love +". A cool breeze blew through the screen door as I asked him about Grandma. He smiled as he reflected on their life together but his eyes told a different story, one of longing. He had spent the last 22 years of his life without her love, and missed her dearly. Throughout this interview and several others in the weeks that preceded and followed, Grandpa peppered in stories about Grandma Liz. She was small in stature but played a large roll in his life and those of their children and grandchildren.

He began to describe their courtship which stretched for years; from their time at Dalton Vocational High School through separate moves to Kansas City after graduation. They were friends first and one fateful day changed their path forever, blasting Grandpa James to the top of the list of suitors - at least for her grandparents. Grandpa launched into an epic tale that rivals those of medieval times; one of a knight defending a fair maiden. As the story goes, a suitor named Preston, from Rock Island, IL had come-a-courtin' to Salisbury, MO in search of Grandma, and Grandpa wasn't having any of that. Read along below after scanning the code to listen to the scoop on what happened.

Grandpa and the Rock Island Suitor

"She had a, they had a house party. And it was a guy there from Rock Island, Illinois, that liked her. So he had, he had been drinkin' some. Naturally I didn't drink. I hadn't, I had only gotten drunk one time and that was my 15th birthday. I didn't drink nothin' before or nothin' since. I haven't yet and I'm 94! See, so what happened he told me to come outside and I'll whoop you. I said, 'Okay.' So we went outside, and I went out first. And when he stepped out there I downed him see, I cheated on him. Beat him up, and it was so quiet till I got a chance to beat him, kick him, and do a lot before the people realized what was going on see, at the party. So I didn't go back in the house. I just come on, got in my car, my daddy's car, and come on home."

Grandpa went home and told his parents what happened. The following day they had a heart-to-heart with Grandma's family, explaining to them that alcohol was only an issue for one of the two men, and not Grandpa James. After what was described as radio silence on the telephone line, he was forgiven and invited to return to their house on future occasions.

Grandpa was fiercely protective of Grandma's reputation and they formed a solid friendship built on mutual admiration and humor. It was a combination of her persuasion and his desire to impress that led to the capture of the wild hog and its subsequent release within the school building. They were two peas in a pod, with other peas, soon to be separated.

Grandma moved west to Kansas City with her family, while Grandpa traveled even further west to Salina, KS to build airbases. Eventually he moved to Kansas City with one of his brothers and soon found himself reconnecting with Grandma. He used to travel across the river from 21st & Charlotte in Kansas City, MO where he was staying, to her grandparents' home near 5th & Parallel in Kansas City, KS. Their reconnection was strong and in time their good friendship grew into love.

A photo to Grandpa James from Grandma Liz

With the draft of World War II looming, they got married. After only six months of wedlock, Grandpa's number was pulled. He was off to the United States Army - like it or not.

She gave birth to their first born son while Grandpa was away at training and soon after his return they expanded their family. Their love produced eight beautiful children, James Jr., Verne, Linda, Frances, Terry, Cecelia, Anita, and Kevin; an even split - 4 boys and 4 girls. Each and every one of them brought friends into the fold who became more like surrogate family members. Grandma Liz and Grandpa James took care of everyone as though they were blood relatives. Any friends and neighbors that you meet today will confirm that thought. They were part of the Robinson's family.

There was even a time when one of the neighbor's children was injured severely enough that it warranted a trip to the hospital. Grandpa shared with me how he scooped him up and carried him to the car in a rush. When they arrived at the hospital they found that they were unable to seek treatment as Grandpa had honestly answered the question, "are you his parent?" They zoomed to the next hospital and when asked the same question, the answer was yes. Not just because he needed to answer this way for treatment, but also because they truly were like family.

He was determined to provide for his family (blood and Troup Ave.) the best way he knew how. While he wasn't always available to spend time with his own children, he was still aware of the

Grandpa James and Grandma Liz with all 8 children

young adults they were growing into. When I asked him to describe what his children were doing today his chest swelled with pride. "They are all educated, and that's important!" All eight of his children attended college and were all doing well. He provided a snapshot of each life.

On His Children

Jim: the first born child whose life had run its course just a few short years ago, was resilient in pushing through the residual effects of the Vietnam War to build a life with his own family; wife and Frances and their daughter Stacey.

Verne: the second born child who pursued a career in Milling Science, and started a family of his own; wife Sylvia, son Roy, and me, their daughter.

Linda: the first daughter and third born child with multiple advanced degrees, who committed her life to helping others around the country and supporting her step-son, Cory.

Frances: the second daughter and fourth born child who regularly checks in on him from Houston, TX and runs their family owned business with daughters Anita, and Shari, while Lurlean and Larry pursued careers outside of their engineering firm.

Terry: the third boy and fifth born child, who traveled overseas while working in the field of architecture before returning home to rebuild and strengthen Robinson's Delivery Service.

Cecelia: the third girl and sixth born child, who pursued a career in both the banking and insurance industries, while also building a family with husband Frank; enter their children Lewis, Ryan, and Robyn.

Anita: the fourth girl and seventh born child, who forged into a leadership role within Robinson's Delivery Service before fearlessly charting a new career path.

Kevin: the fourth boy and eighth born child who can fix or build anything, served in a leadership role within Robinson's Delivery Service, and is husband to Danita.

As he discussed his children there was an ever present mile-wide smile and glow that surrounded him. He was tickled to talk about his newest family members; grandchildren's spouses and his great-grandchildren.

For Grandpa James, home was in his heart and just as his physical home was filled with family, so grew his capacity to love. There was no line between friends and family. His friendships grew as deep as those with his siblings, children and wife.

One of his lifelong friends, Chuck Moore, fell into this group of chosen family members. He and Chuck served with each other in World War II and were a strong support for each other. But his friendship with Chuck started in basic training in Texas.

Listen as Grandpa James tells us more about the start of his friendship with Chuck Moore and a few other guys.

Grandpa James and the Watermelon

"They would come, then in the evening we'd get finished. Let's go downtown, we had about a mile or so from town, and get a watermelon. So I went with 'em once. And so here a month or so later, 'We goin' to get another watermelon. You goin'?' I says, 'No, I don't wanna go, I don't wanna go.' Them d*mn boogers went down there and got the watermelon, brought it back out there to eat so I could eat with 'em. They took a gunnysack and put it in there, HA!! Yeah, but that's what you'd, you was close. I said, 'No, I don't wanna go out there with y'all.' Sheeee, they took a sack with them and got there, went down there and got their, walked down there - see you had to walk, ain't no ridin' there. You had to walk. And uh, and got the watermelon and brought it back out there. 'Hey James, we got the watermelon!' I said, 'WHAT?' 'Yeah, come on!' There we cut it in four pieces. Yeah, cut it in four pieces."

In the same manner as his buddy Chuck had been sure to take care of Grandpa, bringing the watermelon to back to him, Grandpa was sure to take care of him as well, encouraging him to bring back as much money from the war as possible so he could start fresh. They looked after each other growing up, during wartime, and as they both began building their individual families. This kind of support lasted throughout Grandpa's 50 + years of marriage and was present during and after the passing of Grandma Liz. Chuck Moore was there for Grandpa just as his natural born family was. Grandpa's extension of respect was returned when needed, without question.

That's what's important, a level of love that allows you to see beyond any self-imposed barriers and into the heart of another. It is love and friendship and empathy and regard and solidarity and harmony and understanding and good will all rolled into one hard to define explanation; love +. That's the type of love that Grandpa

James shared with Grandma Liz, their children and countless friends and extended family.

According to Grandpa,

"...it's got to be a part of you."

Love + is embedded within you and everyday you have a new chance to share what's important with those around you.

Chapter 9
On Happiness

During each interview, Grandpa consistently wore a broad-faced smile when discussing three general areas; Dalton, his family, and anything related to singing. Vocal music wove a continuous thread throughout his life, stitching together his existence across planes - from his youth through life today.

He spoke a bit about the significance of the music selected to exalt the name of Jesus on Sundays and how each song held a greater message.

Grandpa James on the Songs of Church

>"Even in church, the way they passed the messages was through song. You wouldn't just sit out and have a

meeting and talk and this'n that. You just sang and passed the word and that was it."

Using his voice to send a message was a notion that Grandpa enjoyed tremendously. When the opportunity arose to sing in high school, he was more than ready to join the choir. While sharing the experiences he had traveling to choral competitions with Dalton Vocational High School, a smile appeared that made the crows feet dance around his eyes.

Grandpa James and the Choral Competition

"We had a singing contest. And the first part of that singing contest, it was done at Lincoln University. And the first part of it, all the schools got together and had certain songs. The bases was in this corner. The baritones was in this, you know. Everybody from every school was separated then after that you separated in your own school, and then you do your singing, see. And uh, they would uh, I can remember one, one uh song was 'Fairest Lord Jesus'. Now I don't know...that's the one I remember, but, as I go through or if I hear one at church I can remember those songs there, see. Now we're talkin' about back in the 30s. See, we're talking about back in the 30s - 32 or 3 or somethin' like that. Uh huh, yeah, we was back in the 30s."

When he suddenly found himself in the Army, the presence of music surprisingly remained. He shared with me how he had the opportunity to view one of the U.S.O. shows from backstage. The theatrics of it all fascinated him.

Grandpa James and The Shuffle Along

"The Lieutenant we had, Martin was his name. He says, 'We goin' to The Shuffle Along tonight y'all.' And so, it was at a hotel where they had the show and everything. We went in where the show people was. Now, you would be surprised how they changed clothes. Now the women would have on, just covered here and here, and they'd come in and somebody would take that off and another one'd put that on. Then back out there they would go! Yeah! Ole Martin, he had invited them out to our camp on their days off so we were a part of The Shuffle Along. And, it was out of New York. It was a, it was a U.S.O. show out of New York. Shuffle Along. So if you ever see it or anywhere, anything where they mention Shuffle Along, that was the one. Yeah."

"So what kind of numbers did they do?"

"Everything. Dancing and singing and everything. Yeah, oh yeah. Some would Jitterbug. Some would do just the Charleston. And then they would have talking things that they would, you know, little shows where they would talk and everything. And Martin, he was our Lieutenant, he invited us, invited 'em out to our camp on their days off. And we'd cook a big dinner for them and everything."

Music during the war provided a reprieve for soldiers who were regularly exposed to sights and experiences that were pretty bleak. It was extremely important for them to find a beacon of happiness through these adverse times and Grandpa was fortunate to have connected with the *Shuffle Along* gang.

After returning home from war, Grandpa filled his life with family and music. As they grew taller and wiser, his children learned to play instruments and sing just as he had as a youngster. Continuing the circle of praise that began in Dalton, they regularly sang in church and school choirs growing up in Kansas City, KS. They filled his house with music and all the joy that accompanies it. As each child matured and left for college, music remained a constant in Grandpa's life. Once all had left the nest, he and Grandma traveled more, roaming from location to location.

Grandpa James and Grandma Liz on vacation

Eventually their travels led them to the big island, Hawaii. While he and Grandma Liz journeyed to Hawaii in their retirement, Grandpa had also packed music along for the ride.

Grandpa shared a story with me about his cruise debut, a duet with the ship's crew.

Grandpa and the Hawaii Serenade

"We went on our anniversary one time and then with, with a group the second time. We went, had the cruise the second time, and we went to all the islands. And each night on the ship they would have a talent program. And different ones would try to do different stuff and whatnot. And we didn't, I didn't do nothin' and Lloyd Jones didn't do nothin'. We just stayed out of it. So, after we was 'bout ready to come home we went by, in Hawaii you have the eat places is outside a lot of time. You got inside but everything is you know, it's outside. And we was out there and a guy was walkin' round singing with his mic, 'Goin' to St. Louis'. And he stuck it under my nose and I, he heard my voice. 'Hey,' he says, 'you keep that one. Let me go get another one.' And then Lloyd Jones and I was on to that one. And when we got through singing different songs and everything, the people that was traveling with us fussed at us because we didn't do anything on the ship. I said, 'Well, we didn't come for no talent on the ship. We just came for the ride see.' And all of us that was with that bunch at that eat place, they didn't charge us anything for it. We got it free."

It was a moment that seemingly took over his spirit, music rising from Grandpa like a phoenix. There is a soul-smile that has emanated from every pore in his body in each instance that I've witnessed his singing. I once watched as he enjoyed the musical stylings of a mariachi band in San Antonio, and the joy began to radiate from his skin. Before we knew it, the band had maneuvered closer and Grandpa began to sing along, not knowing a lick of Spanish.

Joy cannot be contained and will often find its way of escaping when we're not paying attention. Finding it is essential to making contact with the toughest curveballs that life throws our way. Grandpa James still sings when he can in the Men's Chorus at his church home. It provides a break from the regular routine and an opportunity to liken back to his childhood while remaining present in the current year. Even though his physical ability has shifted that hasn't stopped him from doing what makes him happy.

"Sometimes when they sing I just stay up in the stand, but I still sing."

While Grandpa doesn't always feel up to standing, it does not stop his love of singing.

Grandpa James outside his church home.

Happiness will continue to flow when you persist through shifting conditions. While its presence may not be felt at all times, I assure you it still resides within your soul. Your job is to recall those things which bring you joy, to summon happiness from its slumber and provide a space for it to live.

Chapter 10
On Life's Journey

Ninety-four years on this earth can throw you a lot of curveballs. That's a lot of living, surviving, and when you claim it, a lot of thriving. Grandpa credits his 94 years of life to a handful of things. One of which was not smoking or drinking (except once when he was 15). The strongest of these was his faith.

It burgeoned from birth. He was born into a religious family, both grandfathers Baptist preachers. His family attended church regularly and faith was embedded in Grandpa's fiber.

- QR Code on next page -

Grandpa James and His Faith

"See, I was raised in a religious family. And so that's all we ever knew. You know, we was, and anytime you're raised that way, it's got to be a part of you. You see. It's just like, I told the preacher, this new preacher we got, I told him, I says, 'Reverend, I want you to know that my medicine costs me so much money now, 'til I don't have enough money on a pension to do at church like I should.'

He said, 'Brother Robinson, I understand that. Everybody at church should know that after a certain length of time, if you're not working, you don't have, some things you can give and some things you can't. Don't you worry 'bout that. Don't you even think about that. 'Cause over the years, you have put enough here to keep this church going.'

And so that's the reason that I was just the religion I was.

And raised from a religious family, it wasn't no problems see. No problems."

Being a man of faith helps Grandpa understand what it means to acknowledge your existence within a purpose driven life. Understanding that you were meant to be in the very spot you are in right now, is understanding part of your purpose. Each step forward, each step back, it all builds upon itself to ensure you are right where you need to be to learn, grow, and help others do the same.

This was ever important as Grandpa James found himself in a situation that would require his mental and physical preparation to help others. Find out more about this slippery situation in the next story.

Grandpa James and the Icy Road

"So okay, we would come, we would ride him downtown

(the streetcar). We'd catch a bus, the one that took us to Fairfax. Well it took us to 4th & Minnesota. That's the Quindaro bus, 4th & Minnesota. Then we catch a bus at 4th & Minnesota. One morning it was slick, and we got off the Quindaro bus. There was a lady, young lady, 'bout you know our ages, was in our neighborhood, that worked in the cafeteria down at that place. She fell. Here's the bus comin' down on her. He couldn't stop 'cause it was ice on there, see. He was slidin'. My buddy, Cag, he tried to get her. He fell. That's two of 'em there. And the bus still comin'. I hit both of 'em and we slid up on the sidewalk. And we was out of sight of the driver. Now that's how close we was! But I could see they was gonna get run over, so I said - sheee - I just, when I just run and just fell with 'em and just knocked them up on the sidewalk. The bus driver, he didn't, it took him a while to get ready to go again. He was, it scared him so."

He approached the entire situation with humility. As though he had not just spared the lives of three people. To him, he was only acting in the manner as he was taught, doing what needed to be done and just moving on. Grandpa's life was the truth personified. For him there was no need to get up in arms about something. In his mind there was always more he could do. Complacency did not take up residence within him.

- QR Code on next page -

Grandpa James and What Else

"But, I was always in on a little bit, try a little bit. I never was, I never did, well I guess I was about as good as you come, but, I never did, never did feel that I was doing my best. I always thought it was a little bit more that I could do."

For Grandpa, keeping this thought in mind allowed him to march forward in life. The same sentiment also allowed him to choose grace in times of challenge. When drafted into the army he didn't like a day of service, but he didn't travel through life with a chip on his shoulder. He just went on.

When he encountered a situation with a mail carrier and needed to investigate the situation, he shared a bit of wisdom with the homeowner,

"Ugly folks, do ugly things. "

It is your job to move beyond that. Doing so requires a deliberate choice to rise above their ugly actions. Again it is that first gem that we referenced in Chapter 1 - On Childhood, that has found its way back to the forefront. Regardless of your challenge at the moment, just go on. That is part of life's journey; walking in faith, understanding a purpose driven life, continued growth instead of stagnation, and choosing grace in unfavorable situations.

Grandpa James prepares to throw out the 1ˢᵗ pitch on his 90th birthday.

So Okay...

Grandpa James has lived a life full of love, learning, loss, gains, and growth. His life is perfectly imperfect, just as it should be. In life, we often wish to walk the most direct path but many times that's not the journey we are intended to take. We fight against the current without realizing that our fight only keeps us in the same place until we cease.

Every day that he's with us is a treasure. Whether you know it or not, someone else also sees a treasure within you. Enjoy the journey. Appreciate the destination. Live with purpose, and lift as you climb.

Epilogue
On Leaving a Legacy

Just less than a month had elapsed between our last interview and Thanksgiving of 2016. During that window of time I was preparing to release another children's book and was allowing some time for grandpa's story to marinate a bit.

His smile was the same as it was when I last saw him and reflected his excitement to spend time with his family. A houseful of people gave him another opportunity to tell more stories. I smiled at my dad as Grandpa launched into tale after tale at dinner. These were documented and soon his legacy would outlast us all.

So okay...after clearing the table from dinner, our family separated into different areas of the house to watch tv, snack on some of the leftovers, or just reconnect with each other. A few of us remained upstairs within eyesight of Grandpa.

My cousin and I had planned to wear very similar shirts to dinner. Hers describing a fabricated quote from Rosa Parks, "Nah." Mine, detailing an assumed statement by Harriet Tubman, "We out."

Our entire family is full of witty wisecrackers, and they got a kick out of our shirts. Simultaneously they acknowledged the gravity and timeliness of each message; 45 having just been elected a few weeks prior. Our nation was having an identity crisis and now more than ever in my lifetime you could hear the voice of dissent.

Some protested quite vocally, other protests were more subdued. While we were mostly joking, my cousin and I were both inherently aware of their relevance on the state of our existence within today's America. We took a few pictures to document the moment and let it simmer down.

I joined Grandpa in the living room and he asked me what we

were doing over there. I told him that people were laughing about our shirts. "What's it say?" he asked. I told him. He burst with the laughter of a proud grandfather, saying between chuckles, "I got a shirt!" My mom, who was sitting nearby, asked what he said. He snickered some more as he unbuttoned his sweater vest and repeated a bit louder, "I got a shirt!"

My grandfather proceeded to peel back each side of his button-up shirt, à la Superman, to reveal a cotton t-shirt with the trifecta of black thought leaders. "Y'all got shirts! I got one too." I glanced at his shirt and did a double-take, just like a cartoon character. My mom and I locked wide-eyed stares, our mouths agape in wonder. I called to my cousin to join us.

My grandpa didn't just have a shirt. He had the shirt; Malcom X, Frederick Douglass, and Dr. William Edward Burghardt (W.E.B.) DuBois.

It was right there all along, hiding in plain sight, behind his Alaska suspenders and conservative outfit. Grandpa's activism was stealthy in its existence, ever present and ready to go at a moment's notice. He had stunned us all into a fit of "I can't believe this just happened" laughter.

"Sometimes I wear this to church, underneath my shirt! You never know what I have on under here," he said beaming with pride.

Here's Grandpa with the two of us on Thanksgiving day, 2016.

Throughout his life, his children and grandchildren have watched his example. We inherited his blood and along with it, his spirit of persistence. We work to improve our world, one person, one child at a time. That takes a village of thoughtful, deliberate, and committed adults, willing to set an strong example for those coming behind.

Our legacy, like Grandpa's, will live on in the generations that follow. They're watching right now and our actions are the outline for our life story. How will you be remembered on childhood, on education, on work & discipline, on challenge & errors, on courage, on family, on connection, on what's important, on happiness, and on life's journey?

It's yours to choose.

CPSIA information can be obtained
at www.ICGtesting.com
Printed in the USA
LVOW08*1102040817
543682LV00005B/15/P